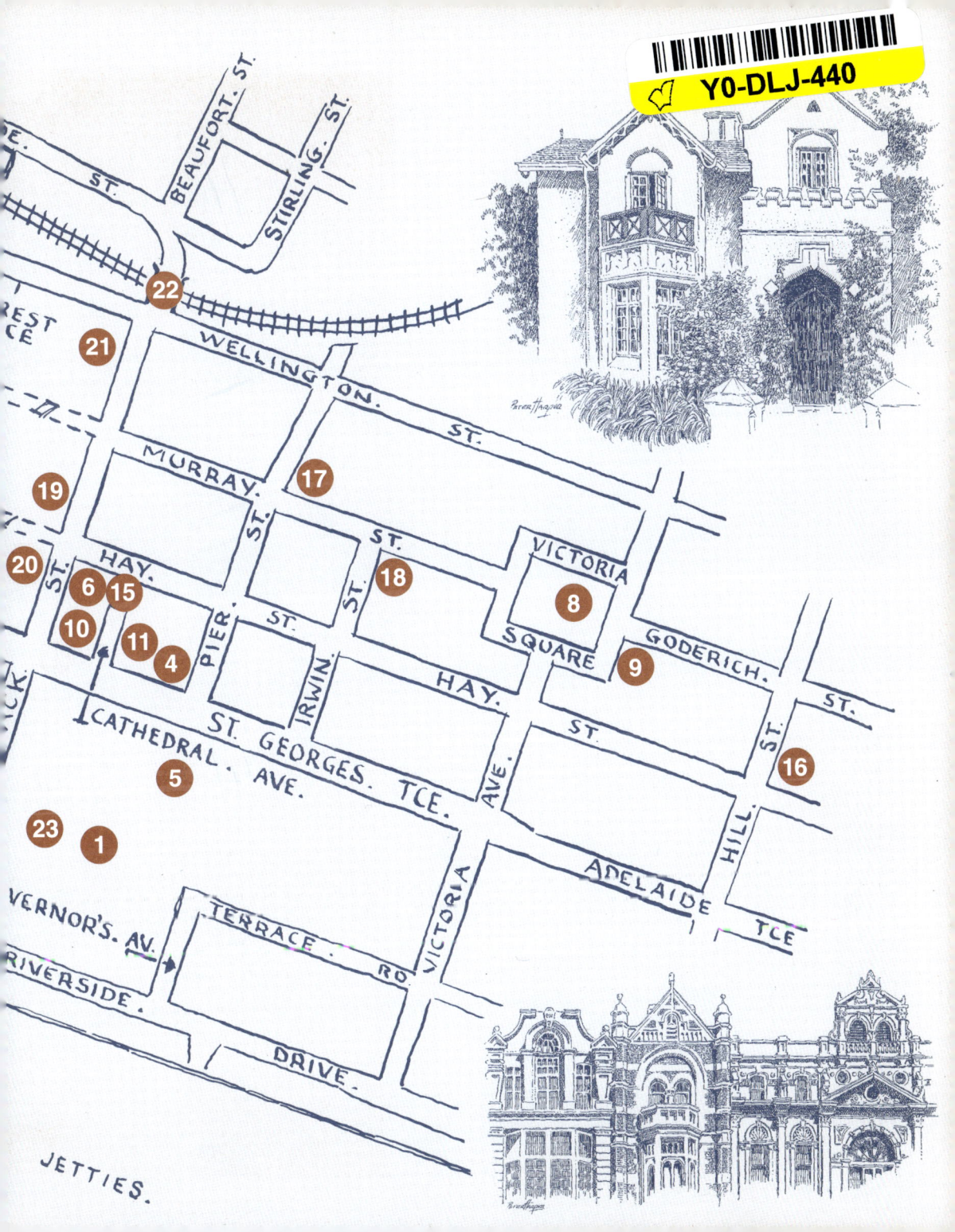

PERTH SKETCHBOOK

PERTH SKETCHBOOK

BARRY STRICKLAND & PETER HARPER

University of Western Australia Press

First published in 1995 by
University of Western Australia Press
Nedlands, Western Australia 6009

This book is copyright. Apart from any fair dealing for the purpose of private study, research, criticism or review, as permitted under the Copyright Act 1968, no part may be reproduced by any process without written permission. Enquiries should be made to the publisher.

© Barry Strickland & Peter Harper 1995

National Library of Australia
Cataloguing-in-Publication entry:

Strickland, Barry (Barry Wayne).
    Perth sketchbook.

    ISBN 1 875560 40 8.

    1. Historic buildings — Western Australia — Perth — Guidebooks. 2. Perth (WA) — History. 3. Perth (WA) — Pictorial works. 4. Perth (WA) — Buildings, structures, etc. — Guidebooks. I. Harper, Peter, 1934– . II Title.

    994.11

Consultant Editor: Amanda Curtin, Curtin Communications, Perth
Designed by Susan Ellvey of Designpoint
and Robyn Mundy, Mundy Design, Perth
Typeset in 10pt Tiffany by Lasertype, Perth
Printed by Scott Four Colour Print, Perth

CONTENTS

WALKING MAP OF PERTH — Endpapers

INTRODUCTION — 1

	Sketch	*Description*
BRICK BY BRICK: 1829–1869		
Old Court House	5	3
The Cloisters	7	12
Bishop's House	9	12
The Deanery	11	12
Government House	13	16
Perth Town Hall	15	16
Wesley Church	17	20
St Mary's Cathedral	19	20
WAITING FOR GOLD: 1870–1891		
Mercy Convent	21	26
Central Government Offices	23	28
St George's Cathedral	25	28

	Sketch	Description
GOLD! GOLD! GOLD! 1892–1900		
Weld Club	27	34
Trinity Church	29	34
Former Palace Hotel	31	36
Titles Office	33	38
Royal Mint	35	38
Former Government Printing Office	37	40
Former Central Fire Station	39	40
Former Albany Bell Tea Rooms	41	42
Barrack Street facades	43	42
Former Seeligson Loan Office	45	44
Barrack Street Bridge	47	44
SETTLING INTO PROSPERITY: 1901–1910		
Supreme Court	49	46
His Majesty's Theatre	51	50
20 Howard Street	53	52
NOTES		55

INTRODUCTION

The older Perth gets, the younger it looks. The shining towers of commerce proclaim that this is a city of today and tomorrow. Yesterday was (and always will be) another world.

When you look at a map it is obvious that the Western Australian capital is a long way from anywhere. Much has been made of this geographic isolation. It has been used as a defence and as an excuse for what the city is and is not.

Perth faces west across a sandy sliver of coastline. The beaches are the city's front yard. Out the back is a hilly ridge that masks the beginning of a vast, largely empty interior. From the front porch, with the afternoon sun dipping deep into the Indian Ocean beyond Rottnest, the focus is firmly out to sea. It is a sea that has been closely observed since European settlement began in 1829.

When novelist Anthony Trollope paid Perth a visit in 1872, he found 'a very pretty town, built on a lake of brackish water formed by the Swan River'. But the service he experienced at his inn was less than he had hoped for: 'the people seemed to be too well off to care for strangers'.[1] Perhaps Trollope was experiencing a certain independence of spirit (and a disdain for kowtowing to outsiders) that has been discernible from the earliest of days.

Trollope was correct to note the city's site on the banks of the Swan River. Not to do so would be tantamount to ignoring Sydney's harbour. The Swan is gracious rather than grand. By the time it has eased down the Darling Scarp and found itself on the coastal plain, it has decided to be old. It has slowed and spread itself out in a most agreeable configuration.

When Governor Stirling chose the Swan's northern bank (just a curve to the east of a narrow, defendable 'neck') as the site for the new colony's chief city, he did so partly with an eye to the beauty of the spot. It was a location that had probably been admired by Willem de Vlamingh in 1696 and was certainly the subject of a French diary entry in 1801 (members of the exploratory expedition being 'charmed with a beautiful prospect'[2]). Today, when viewed from Kings Park, the site still has the power to charm. Within the scene's wide frame are three distinct elements set against the blue-green contours of the Darling Scarp: the city skyline, the lake-like expanse of Perth Water, and the Narrows Bridge arching to meet the South Perth peninsula.

In the 165 years or so that it has taken Perth to grow into a youthful metropolis, spreading itself Los Angeles–style along the narrow coastal plain, its city streets have been shaped by optimistic free settlers, consolidated by convicts, reshaped by gold, and further transformed by an entrepreneurial spirit that had its birth in mountainous blocks of iron ore.

PERTH SKETCHBOOK

Brick by brick: 1829–1869

Old Court House
Sketch p. 5

Perth's built environment reveals many tales. Take, for instance, the city's 'colonial heart', the precinct of government and church buildings surrounding Stirling Gardens. This was where the first tents were pitched in August 1829, and it is here that you will find Perth's oldest surviving structure, the former **Court House**. Erected in 1836 and officially opened with a church service on Good Friday 1837, the old Court House is tucked away in the south-east corner of the site. The building has a gentle visual appeal that belies a lively history of use by both Church and State. It is essentially a rectangular box conforming to the Georgian sense of proportion, to which has been added a simple porch with rather squat Doric columns — not a building upon which its architect, Henry Willey Reveley, could hope to build a reputation, but certainly one that has aged gracefully.

In the early years of settlement, any building with four solid walls and a good roof was a rarity. The Court House provided both, and because crime in the fledgling colony was infrequent, there were always going to be other demands on its usage. Apart from its official designation, it served as a place of worship, education and entertainment. This eclectic mix created some tensions in the community, but Perth's small population could not yet hope to enjoy a full range of purpose-built facilities.

A legendary story associated with the old Court House is that of the fund-raising piano recital given by Father Dom Salvado, the Benedictine monk who arrived with three colleagues at the Swan River early in 1846. Salvado's mission was to bring Christian care and values to the Aborigines of the Bolgart district north-east of Perth. After a couple of months spent in a successful search of the tribal groups the monks were to minister to, their supplies had run out and support from Perth had to be urgently secured if the mission was to survive.

With an Aboriginal companion and guide, Salvado undertook the arduous 160 kilometre walk back to Perth, only to be told by Bishop Brady that he and his brothers would have to abandon their mission because the colony's tiny Catholic community did not possess the means to support it. Salvado took this as a challenge and, being an accomplished musician, he suggested that a public recital might be the way to secure the necessary funds.

After Salvado had finished his three-hour performance at the Court House on 21 May 1846, he had succeeded, through keyboard dexterity, in uniting Perth's Catholic, Anglican and Jewish citizens to his cause. The press observed that 'it is much to be regretted that Mr. Salvado should resign himself to a bush life where his eminent talents must be wasted; it is a serious

---

Old Court House, 1836–37
Stirling Gardens, off Barrack Street
Architect: Henry Willey Reveley

loss to the community, and we seriously apprehend that his enthusiasm in the cause he has undertaken will be ill requited'.[3]

But not even the story of the concert that helped to make the Benedictine mission at New Norcia a bit of Old Spain in a young country can quite compete with that of the Court House's architect, Reveley.

Reveley's arrival with Stirling on the *Parmelia* in 1829 can be put down to fate. He was, ostensibly, the quintessential Englishman abroad. He had a modestly famous father, 'Athenian' Reveley (who had helped bring about English architecture's Classical Revival during George III's long reign), and a vivacious and cultured mother, Maria. Included in his parents' somewhat radical circle of friends were the feminist Mary Wollstonecraft and her philosopher husband, William Godwin. When Wollstonecraft died within days of giving birth to a daughter, Maria Reveley nursed the infant, the future Mary Shelley, wife of Percy and author of *Frankenstein*.

Mary Shelley was to re-enter Reveley's life in 1818, shortly after he had graduated from the University of Pisa as an engineer and was living near Leghorn in Italy. She was accompanied by husband Percy and stepsister Claire Clairmont. Henry soon found himself enmeshed in the romantic machinations of this literary *ménage à trois*, as well as overseeing the refit of their small canal boat. On the boat's maiden voyage it capsized, and Reveley saved Percy Shelley from drowning in the waters of the Arno.

The Cloisters, 1858
200 St Georges Terrace
Architect: Attributed to Richard Roach Jewell. Renovation, 1972, by Howlett & Bailey

Reveley was not about four years later when another of Shelley's boats succumbed to an angry Mediterranean. This was the year Reveley returned to England and entered the competition for the design of a new London Bridge. Simultaneously, he fell in love with Amelia, the sister of the artist Copley Fielding, and they were married. By 1826, they were living in Cape Town, where Henry had been appointed Civil Engineer for the Cape Province.

With Cape Town being a vital replenishment stop for ships engaged upon the long voyage to the East Indies and New South Wales, Reveley's immediate task was to improve the harbour. But within a year of his arrival, there were charges of professional misconduct against him, and while these were proven to be mischievous, he was not reinstated. Dejected and forced to freelance, all the time seeking to restore his damaged reputation, Reveley's fortunes took an unexpected turn with the arrival of the *Parmelia* and Captain James Stirling. Stirling, bound for the Swan River to pioneer what he hoped would be a great 'agricultural' settlement[4], made an offer for Reveley to join the expedition as Civil Engineer.

After arriving with the 'first fleet', the Reveleys were to spend nine years in Perth, time enough for Henry to design and supervise the construction of the numerous buildings (including the first Government House) that were required for public purposes throughout the colony. The constraints on what Reveley could do reflected the conditions in the colony at large: limited

---

Bishop's House, 1859
Behind 225 St Georges Terrace
Architect unknown; possibly from a pattern book, with the involvement of Richard Roach Jewell

funds, limited access to suitable building materials, and a lack of skilled artisans. He no doubt would have liked to have emulated the three tenets of the architectural Classicism championed by his father ('simplicity, strength and vastness'), but while simplicity was not a challenge, strength and vastness were. One senses in Reveley's work a man frustrated by the colony's genteel poverty, dreaming of the 'society' of his Italian years. He returned to England in 1838, abandoning his career to command a minor stage on the lucrative lecture circuit.

In 1856, another Englishman arrived who was to leave a more permanent mark than Reveley's. He was Matthew Blagden Hale, first Anglican Bishop of Perth. His appointment came in the sixth year of Western Australia's life as a penal settlement, and he was horrified that a formerly free colony had to endure the 'moral disease' of convictism. He wrote pamphlets railing against the system, resulting in several heady encounters with the formidable Governor Hampton. In the climate of the day, Hale's less than Christian attitude towards the convicted felons who had been carted halfway round the world to help save the colony from ruin was understandable. Unlike the farmers of York and the merchants of Perth, who had welcomed the convicts, his livelihood was not dependent on a ready supply of cheap labour. Indeed he could afford to be indignant, being the chief beneficiary of his late father's Gloucestershire estate.

Using his own funds, Hale embarked upon a vigorous building programme that included the city's first secondary

---

The Deanery, 1859
Corner St Georges Terrace and Pier Street
Architect: Attributed to Richard Roach Jewell, in association with the Rev. George Pownall

The Cloisters
Sketch p. 7

Bishop's House
Sketch p. 9

The Deanery
Sketch p. 11

school for boys (The Cloisters, 1858), residences for himself (Bishop's House, 1859) and his Dean (The Deanery, 1859), a home for Aboriginal children, and the Church of St Bartholomew at the East Perth cemetery.

Because his opposition to the convict presence in the colony had been broadcast far and wide, Hale was careful to ensure that not a brick of his boys' school was laid by convict hands. But a year later when he was ready to set about building the two houses, which also stand to this day, non-convict labour was not as readily available. He was forced to take on some ticket-of-leavers[5], rationalizing his decision as a sincere desire to bring about their moral reformation by allowing them daily contact with God-fearing men such as himself and Dean Pownall.

The Cloisters was the building in which dozens of boys from colonial 'society' gained the rudiments of a classical education. As Bishop Hale's Church of England Collegiate School, it served the colony well until 1872. It was the alma mater of many of the men who would go on to dominate the political, legal, commercial and educational life of the colony. A glance at just some of the surnames provides proof: Forrest, Parker, Burt, Wittenoom, Lee Steere, Lefroy, Samson, Bateman, de Burgh, Leeder, Mitchell, Shenton, Chidlow, Bovell, Brockman, Roe, Withers . . .

As most of Western Australia's prominent early settlers came from rural England, it is not surprising that their early efforts to replicate 'home' strongly reflected the Georgian sensibility of

---

Government House, 1859–64
St Georges Terrace
Architects: Capt. E.Y.W. Henderson, in association with James Manning and Richard Roach Jewell

the England in which they had grown up. Bishop's House is typical of the rectangular Georgian houses in which individual proportions and ratios contributed to the harmony of the whole. The verandah came as a belated concession to the West Australian sun, wind and rain.

The Deanery is a significant example of how the architectural pattern books that were available at the time influenced colonial architecture, not just in Western Australia but in many other former British colonies. Richard Roach Jewell and the Rev. George Pownall, to whom the building's design is attributed, may well have leafed their way through J.C. Louden's *Encyclopaedia of Cottage, Farm and Village Architecture* (1833) before devising this variation on what was already a romantic theme for small houses 'back home'. Another common source of inspiration was the *Illustrated London News*.

When Dr John Hampton took up his post as Governor of Western Australia in 1862, he arrived with a dubious record in colonial administration, and he certainly was not the kind of man who would be found gladly taking tea with 'the good Bishop'. While Comptroller-General of Convicts in Tasmania, he had been censured for having derived profit from the labours of the prisoners. It was a charge he fought with characteristic vigour. But the greatest blemish on Hampton's character was the fact that he was a friend and ally of bad, mad John Price.

Price was the commandant of the convict establishment on Norfolk Island. He was a great, bull-necked, bow-legged ogre of

---

Perth Town Hall, 1867–70
Corner Hay and Barrack Streets
Architects: Richard Roach Jewell, in association with James Manning

a man whom Marcus Clarke used as the model for the villainous Maurice Frere in *For the Term of His Natural Life*. When allegations of Price's arbitrary and sadistic abuse of convicts began to surface in Tasmania, Hampton wrote a whitewashing report and later tried to discredit all those who continued to raise objections to his colleague's tyrannical rule.

In *The Fatal Shore*, Robert Hughes describes Hampton as a 'dismally cynical opportunist'[6], and his governorship as 'odious and corrupt'.[7] He certainly knew how to work the convict system, and the threat of the lash resonated in the minds of the men who laboured over the most comprehensive programme of public works Western Australia had seen. Among the projects either finished or started during his governorship were three of Perth's finest colonial buildings: **Government House (1859–64)**, the Pensioner Barracks (1867), of which only the arch survives, and the **Perth Town Hall (1867–70)**.

Government House
Sketch p. 13

Perth Town Hall
Sketch p. 15

It is ironic that the two hardy antagonists Bishop Hale and Governor Hampton should have been the overseers in the creation of Perth's distinctive red-brick heritage. With a couple of exceptions, including Hale's Georgian-style home, the buildings they erected were essentially Tudor Gothic in style, with crenellated parapets, turrets, arches, string courses, decorative quoining, and Flemish bond brickwork[8] creating chequerboards out of contrasting tones of red. Many of the bricks were made with clay from the pits at the eastern end of town (now Queen's Gardens). When stone was required, the obvious

---

Wesley Church, 1867–70
Corner Hay and William Streets
Architect: Richard Roach Jewell. Additions and alterations, 1895, by J.J. Talbot Hobbs

choice was Swan River limestone, most of which came from the Rocky Bay quarry just upstream from Fremantle. Jarrah (or Swan River mahogany as it was then commonly called) was quite widely used on account of it being so tough that even the white ants left it alone. For roofing, sheoak shingles were used, as well as slate. The skilled labour that was in short supply in Reveley's time was now more abundant, and many convict era buildings display a technical sophistication that was previously not possible.

Government House, the design of which is principally attributed to Captain E.Y.W. Henderson, is a jewel in the colonial crown. It is very much a nineteenth-century version of the 'fortified' manor house of Tudor and Jacobean times, the Jacobean influence being especially strong in the convex-concave curve of the six tower caps. There is some conjecture that Sir Charles Barry, the distinguished English architect, may have had a hand in its design. Barry was a close friend of Henderson who, from 1850 to 1863, was the Comptroller-General of the Convict Establishment in Western Australia.

With a clock tower that once dominated the city skyline, Perth's Town Hall has been described as being among that special breed of landmark buildings which 'once seen are not easily forgotten'.[9] Its chief designer was Richard Roach Jewell, working in association with James Manning. It reflects Jewell's penchant for borrowing freely (and often very creatively) from a

---

St Mary's Cathedral, 1863–65 (western section shown)
Victoria Square
Architects: Original design attributed to A.W.N. Pugin as freely interpreted by Brother Ascione. Eastern extension, 1920s, by Michael Cavanagh

variety of sources. In scale and detail, the suggestion is that of the late medieval town halls which took pride of place in the squares of Europe's smaller cities. It originally had an arcaded undercroft formed by Gothic arches that was designed to house the city's market. But in an act of civic vandalism, this was later enclosed, the red brick arcading ultimately being replaced with grey granite. While the result is a serious incongruity of design, colour and texture between the ground and first floors, the Town Hall endures as one of Perth's most distinctive buildings.

As Superintendent of Public Works from 1853 to 1884, Jewell made a significant contribution to Perth's architectural heritage. He was an industrious man, his name being closely associated with at least a dozen of the buildings that survive from the convict era. As suggested by his involvement with the Cloisters and the Deanery, not all of his work was for the government. Just a block to the west of the Town Hall, and completed shortly before it, Jewell's **Wesley Church** (1867–70) is a pleasing but more conventional mix of Gothic devices. Like the Town Hall's tower, Wesley's spire, topped with a metal weathercock, was for many years an unmistakable landmark.

Wesley Church
Sketch p. 17

One of the major buildings of the colonial period that did not involve Hale, Hampton or Jewell was the Roman Catholic **St Mary's Cathedral** (1863–65). Also absent were the otherwise ubiquitous red bricks.

St Mary's Cathedral
Sketch p. 19

Roman Catholicism was undergoing a revival when Victoria came to the throne in 1837, one of its many converts being the architect A.W.N. Pugin, who co-designed London's Houses of

---

Mercy Convent, 1873
Victoria Square
Architect: Attributed to McMahon, a former Irish political prisoner

Parliament with Sir Charles Barry. He rejected Classicism as being the language of paganism and sought to bring back an architecture that was 'grand' and 'sublime'. He found his inspiration in the majestic cathedrals of the Middle Ages, and went on to help pioneer the Gothic Revival that was to be the dominant style for ecclesiastical architecture during the Victorian age. A manic workaholic, Pugin burned himself out and died, quite mad, in 1852. It is believed that one of his many church designs found its way into Perth and was used as the basis for what became St Mary's Cathedral.

If the design did come from Pugin's drawing board, it was probably obtained from his London office some time in 1853 by Bishop Serra (the Spanish Benedictine who had succeeded Bishop Brady as Perth's second Roman Catholic Bishop). As this was after Pugin's death, it may well be that his assistants were either giving away designs or selling them cheaply, when Serra happened to be in London. Whatever the case, the design must have been stashed away in a bottom drawer on Serra's return to Perth, only to be retrieved some ten years later when Bishop Griver asked Brother Ascione to make a start on a cathedral.

When St Mary's was completed early in 1865, it did not have its present spire or any of its other spiky Gothic details. Nor did it have the now somewhat incongruous eastern extension, which was added by Michael Cavanagh in the late 1920s with the intention that it would ultimately envelop the original structure. The Great Depression, perhaps fortuitously, intervened.

Central Government Offices, 1874 – c. 1905
St Georges Terrace, between Barrack Street and Cathedral Avenue
Architects: Richard Roach Jewell, George Temple Poole and John Grainger

Waiting for gold: 1870–1891

Governor Hampton's departure in 1868 coincided with the end of convictism. With the free labour source removed, development of the colony slowed. Unlike Victoria, Western Australia had not yet struck it rich. Gold was not far from the minds of colonial administrators, who actively encouraged prospectors (with the lure of a £5,000 reward) to travel far and wide, in the hope that a major find would supplement Western Australia's limited income from the export of timber and wool. But at that time, Bayley and Ford, who were to do for Western Australia what James Esmond had done for Victoria, were yet to appear on the scene.[10]

The successor to Hampton was an altogether nicer man, Frederick Aloysius Weld. He was the colony's first Roman Catholic Governor and had led an active political life in New Zealand where, in 1864, he went from being Minister for Native Affairs to Premier. But his government was defeated in 1865 and he retired to England to recuperate from ill health. It was there that he was offered the governorship of Western Australia. He arrived in time to oversee the division of the colony into electoral districts, which was leading, tentatively, to the introduction of representative government.

St George's Cathedral, 1879–88
St Georges Terrace, near corner Cathedral Avenue
Architect: Edmund Blacket. Tower design, 1902, by J.J. Talbot Hobbs
Foreground, right, is Burt Memorial Hall (1917), architect George Parry

Weld felt uneasy about being the Governor of a colony whose lands were largely unexplored, and he set about planning for an expedition to open up the interior. He selected John Forrest as its leader. Expeditions such as those undertaken by John Forrest and his brother Alexander made it abundantly clear just how remote Western Australia really was. Weld reacted by cutting the sod for the colony's first railway and by planting the first pole for the telegraph link with South Australia. He also passed an Education Act that brought greater equality in the levels of support given to the schools of the various religious denominations.

Perhaps the greatest beneficiary of Weld's evenhandedness was the Catholic education system. With Victoria Square the spiritual heart of the Catholic Church in Perth, its eastern side was selected as the site for the **Mercy Convent (1873)**. Six Sisters of Mercy (the first to arrive in Australia) had been recruited in Ireland by Father Brady back in 1845. They quickly established schools, which were attended by all denominations, and their new 'mother house', designed by a former Irish political prisoner, featured three steep gables with decorative brickwork. The verandah, generously laced with cast iron, came later.

Mercy Convent
Sketch p. 21

Before Weld departed to take up the governorship of Tasmania, he made provision for a new Treasury Building, to be constructed on the corner of Barrack Street and St Georges Terrace. This was the first stage of what would, some thirty-one years later, become a significant complex of government offices

---

Weld Club, 1892
Corner Barrack Street and The Esplanade
Architect: J.J. Talbot Hobbs

Central Government Offices
Sketch p. 23

incorporating the General Post Office and occupying almost an entire block. These **Central Government Offices (1874 – c. 1905)** were the work of three successive government architects — Richard Roach Jewell, George Temple Poole and John Grainger — each of whom contributed to its shape as it shed its plain 1870s colonial garb to emerge as a Second Empire Parisian dandy.[11]

While Jewell was finishing off the second building in the government complex, next door the Anglican community was preparing to build a cathedral. To do so, it would have to demolish the existing Church of St George (which may have been based on a design Reveley had prepared before he left the colony) and engage a suitable architect. Mindful of the generous scale and prominent position of St Mary's in Victoria Square (a site they had passed up), the Anglicans spent some time considering plans by prominent British architects, before offering the job to Sydney's Edmund Blacket. A leading exponent of the Gothic Revival style, his fame reached its height in 1860 with the completion of the Great Hall at Sydney University, arguably one of Australia's finest buildings.

St George's Cathedral
Sketch p. 25

With over fifty church designs to his credit, Blacket's drawings for **St George's Cathedral (1879–88)** were predicated on a clear understanding that the purse was tight and that expensive structural and stylistic devices such as pier shafting and buttressing would not be possible. Blacket's solution was to draw upon the English Gothic of the early medieval period and to build mostly in brick, with limestone used sparingly for the

---

Trinity Church, 1893
St Georges Terrace
Architect: Henry Trigg

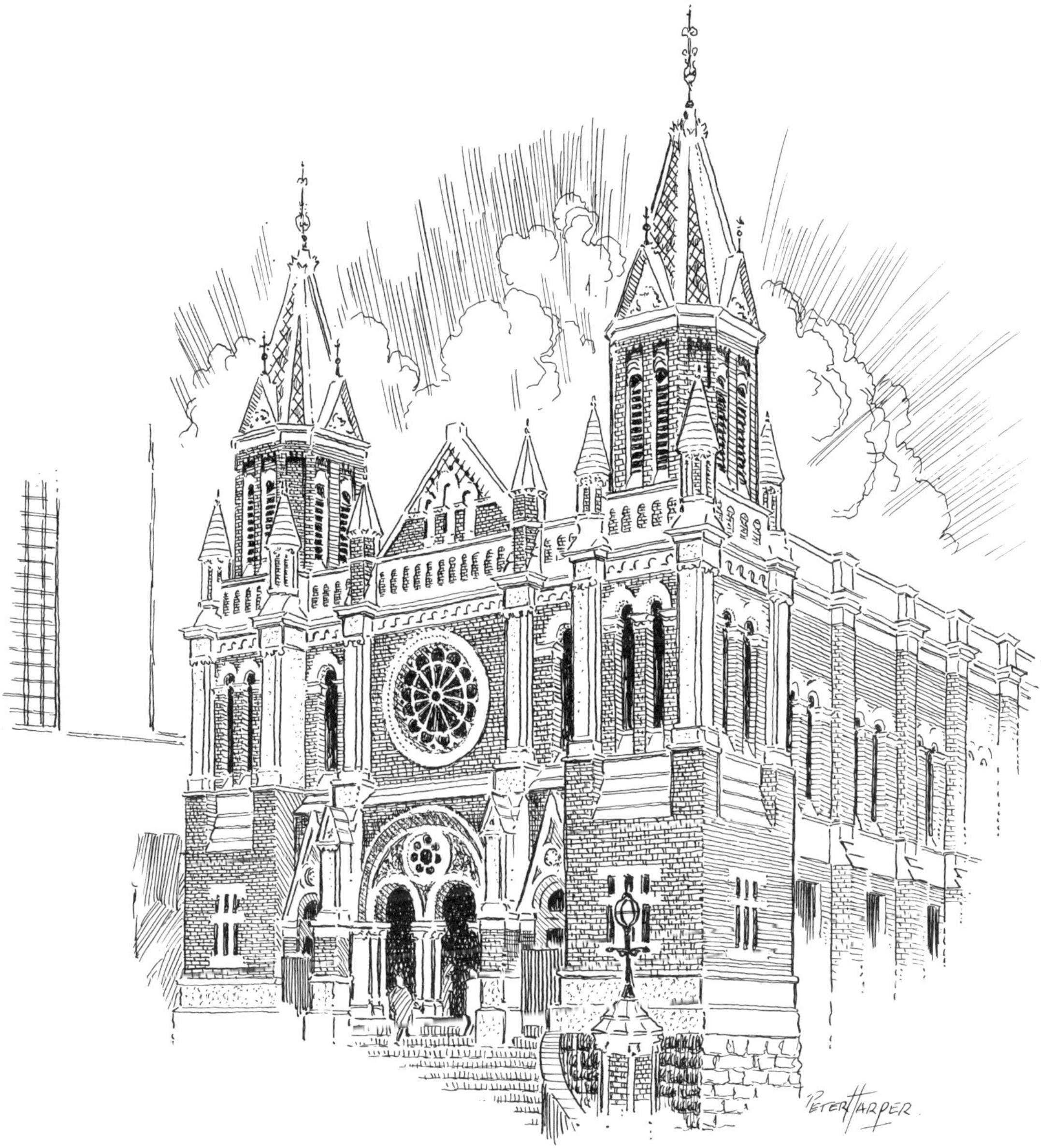
PETER HARPER

windows and bluestone for the nave columns. While Blacket never visited Perth and died while building was still in progress, his son saw to it that the design was closely adhered to. But a lack of funds meant that the spire he had intended was never built. In 1902, the cathedral acquired a square tower, a memorial to the late Queen Victoria.

While St George's Cathedral may be 'less pretentious than the spectacular Gothic cathedrals of Sydney, Melbourne and Adelaide'[12], the interior is undeniably lovely. The jarrah framing of the ceiling provides a rich contrast to the soft warmth of the bricks, while some fine stained glass produces a subtle interior glow. Had the cathedral been built during the gold boom, it would certainly have been, both in scale and style, a very different structure.

Gold! Gold! Gold! 1892–1900

It was the winter of 1892 when Arthur Bayley and William Ford wrote themselves into the history books. At a place they named Fly Flat, deep in desolate scrub country some 550 kilometres east of Perth, they used a tomahawk to break the top off a quartz reef and proceeded to dolly[13] some 500 ounces of gold from the reef. Within weeks, the rush was on. The *West Australian* of 21

Former **Palace Hotel, 1895**
Corner St Georges Terrace and William Street
Architects: Porter & Thomas
The sign above the entrance changed from 'R & I Bank of WA' to 'BankWest' in April 1994

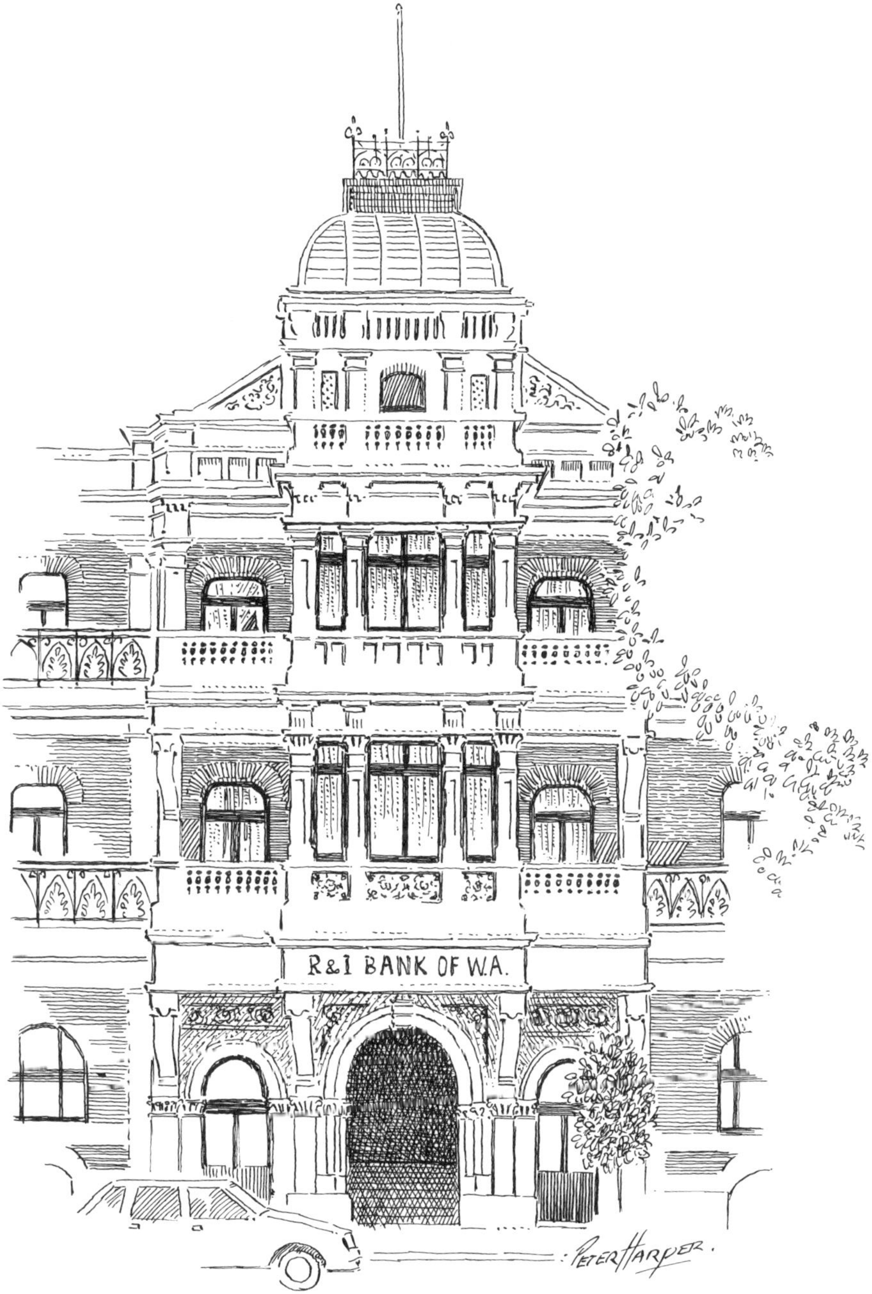
R&I BANK OF W.A.
PETER HARPER.

September reported that 'in Perth and Fremantle everyone seems to be either carrying tents, picks, shovels, and dishes, or otherwise preparing for the road'. And it was not uncommon to see trains of eighty, ninety or a hundred camels, weighed down with provisions, and complaining noisily as they left Perth to start the long trek to the goldfields.

'Gold' was the word on everyone's lips and Western Australia was the talk of the world. After sixty-three years of being a poor relative to its Eastern cousins, Perth was firmly on the map.

In 1892 there were just twelve registered architectural firms in Western Australia. But with the gold discoveries coinciding with the economic recession of the 1890s, there were suddenly architects heading in Perth's direction from all points of the globe. By 1896 there were 102 registered architects in business.

One young architect who was already in Perth when word of the Bayley and Ford bonanza reached the capital was J.J. Talbot Hobbs. Having arrived from England in 1887 (following in the wake of his sweetheart), he was better placed than most to exploit the situation, because, having married the object of his desire, he now had Mr J. Hurst as a father-in-law. Hurst was not only a builder but also a Perth City Councillor. In the free-spending period leading up to 1901, Talbot Hobbs won commissions to design and erect a great many commercial and residential buildings. One source suggests that the total value of the properties he designed was in excess of £750,000.[14] No project was too large or too small for Talbot Hobbs. From imposing office buildings on the Terrace to elegant Federation-

---

Titles Office, 1897 (entrance shown)
Corner Hay Street and Cathedral Avenue
Architect: George Temple Poole

1897

style bungalows in Peppermint Grove, he was to the private sector (in the gold rush days) what George Temple Poole was to the public domain.

Weld Club
Sketch p. 27

Talbot Hobbs's big break came with his winning the design competition for a new **Weld Club** (1892), to be built on the corner of Barrack Street and The Esplanade. His design features a belvedere corner tower, effectively positioned on the diagonal. It was a prestige site, looking south across the Swan, and entirely appropriate for the city's most affluent and influential gentlemen's club. 'The Weld' had been founded in the 1870s, and named in honour of its first patron, Governor Weld. It drew its members exclusively from the moneyed and landed gentry as well as from the higher ranks of the colonial administration and the military. It was, in effect, a London club 'down under'.

Trinity Church
Sketch p. 29

Up on St Georges Terrace, the Congregationalists were building their second **Trinity Church** (1893). The first (which still stands, obscured by the second) had been opened in 1865, with the colony's foremost Congregationalist, Henry Trigg, leading the prayers. In the early years of settlement, Trigg had secured most of the government building contracts, becoming one of the wealthier 'grand old men' of the city. His grandson, also a Henry Trigg, was probably the first locally born architect, and it was he who designed the church of 1893. He did so on a difficult site, filling the space between the facade of the first church and the pavement. The result made the new Trinity very much a 'town church', modest in scale and fitting easily into the

---

Royal Mint, 1896–99 (entrance shown)
Corner Hay and Hill Streets
Architect: George Temple Poole. 1991 restoration by Forbes & Fitzhardinge

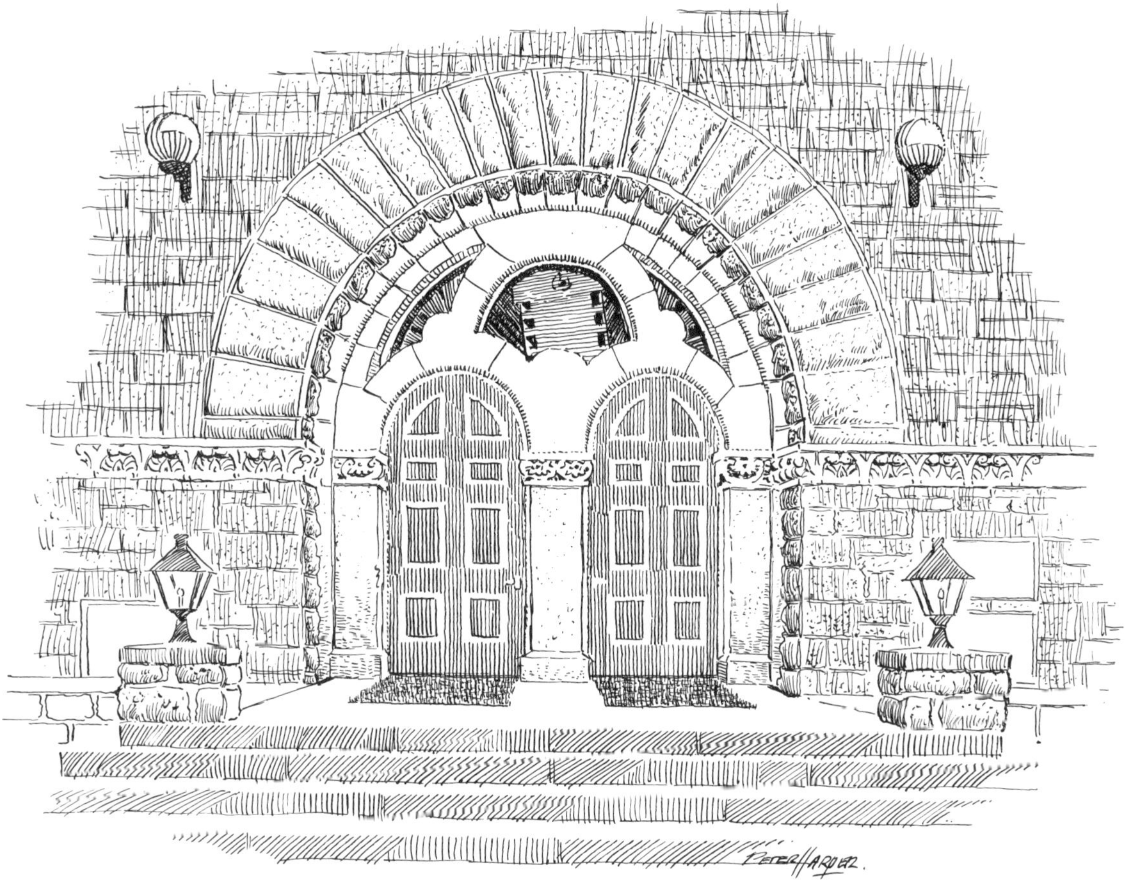
PETER HARPER.

streetscape. While eclectic in its architectural influences, and built from red brick, the composition and symmetry of its parts suggest Trigg may have been a fan of Notre Dame and other masterpieces of the French Gothic.

Palace Hotel
Sketch p. 31

By the mid-1890s, there were so many gold-seekers with thirsts to quench and in need of beds to collapse into that hotels could not be built quickly enough. The **Palace Hotel (1895)** was a particularly sumptuous establishment — and certainly not for the wild boys. Commanding the north-eastern corner of the intersection of William Street and St Georges Terrace, it was the work of the Melbourne-based firm of Porter & Thomas. Every one of its machine-made bricks came by ship from Melbourne: an illustration of just how much money was around at that time. It was built for the Californian-born entrepreneur John de Baun, a somewhat enigmatic figure, it would seem, given that he fails to get a mention in any of the major texts. The architects used a restrained form of the popular French Second Empire style, capping the imposing three-storey facade with an iron-crested square dome upon which a flag was always flown. Today, the Palace is a classic example of the price a city can pay for the preservation of its heritage. Beautifully restored to near-original condition, the former hotel is now a banking chamber, and the elegant dining room, once among the finest in Australia, is an office.

The man who held the post of Colonial Architect and Superintendent of Public Works during the heady gold rush

---

Former **Government Printing Office, 1891–94**
Corner Murray and Pier Streets
Architect: From the office of George Temple Poole, with the involvement of W.B. Hardwick

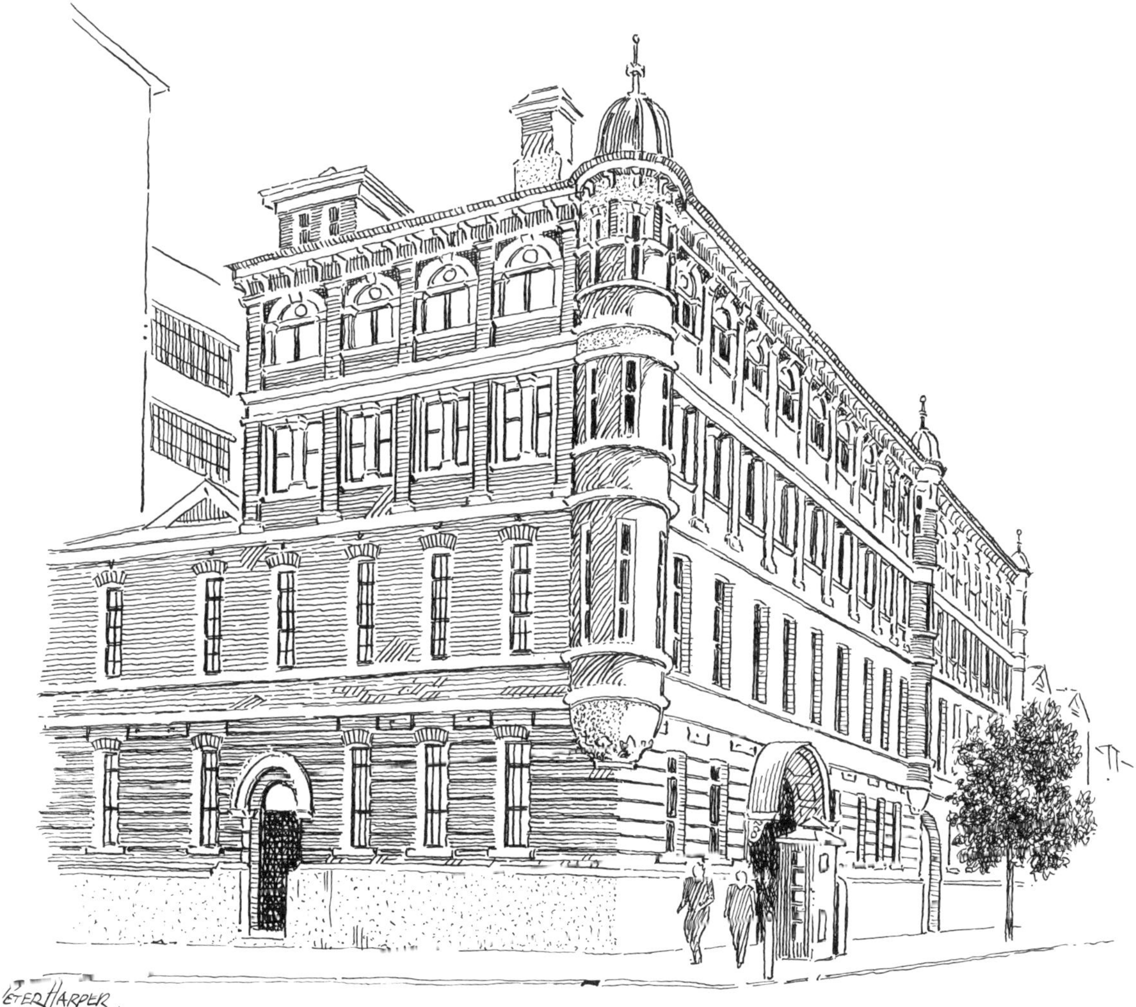
PETER HARPER

years was George Temple Poole. The government, led by John Forrest, was struggling to keep up with the many demands made by a population that was expanding at an alarming rate.[15] All sorts of new facilities and services had to be provided. Temple Poole and his assistants (most notably Robert Haddon) found themselves designing railway stations, lighthouses, schools, post offices and accommodation for the burgeoning public service. From 1885 until 1897, his office was responsible for almost 300 designs.

Many Temple Poole buildings survive. His work is remarkable for its variety, but once you know his idiosyncrasies, such as his fondness for setting entrance ways within generous Romanesque arches, it is difficult to mistake. Perhaps his most memorable work is the **Titles Office** (1897), which represents Temple Poole's most audacious mix of classical devices. The main columns of the suspended double balcony have Corinthian capitals, while the miniature columns in the upper and lower balustrades feature variations on the Ionic and Doric, respectively. An authoritative text on Australian architecture describes this building as 'one of Australia's finest and most dramatic Free Classical buildings'.[16] Another says, 'Poole at his best . . . The close relationship of building to street, generated by overhanging balconies, has a sophistication unequalled in Perth.'[17]

Titles Office
Sketch p. 33

Where Temple Poole's Titles Office is all sweeping elegance, with its bracketed colonnades taking the eye up and along, his design for the Perth branch of the **Royal Mint** (1896–99) is much

Royal Mint
Sketch p. 35

Former **Central Fire Station**, c. 1900 (section of Murray Street facade shown)
Corner Murray and Irwin Streets
Architects: Cavanagh & Cavanagh

FIRE STATION

more muscular. The Rottnest Island limestone used in its construction has been rusticated, and at ground level the series of nine semicircular arches are in the Romanesque manner of the American architect Henry Richardson. Set within the central arch are twin arched doors. With its sensitively handled restoration, the Perth Mint now looks better than ever.

Other notable public buildings constructed during Temple Poole's time as Colonial Architect include the former **Government Printing Office** (1891–94), the former General Post Office (part of the Central Government Office complex), the Old Observatory (actually the former Astronomer's Residence), the Central Railway Station, the old Museum, and the Royal Perth Hospital Administration Building. The old Government Printing Office is one of Perth's more curious structures. The ground and first floors suggest a conservative formality, but with each successive level, the design becomes less inhibited. The upper floors are united by rounded oriel turrets topped with bronze domes.

Government Printing Office
Sketch p. 37

After leaving the government service, Temple Poole went into private practice with C.F. Mouritzen. One of his last buildings, Sheffield House (c. 1929) in central Hay Street, is a design in the style of the 'Chicago School' and provides further proof of the versatility that characterized what was a remarkable fifty-year career.

Central Fire Station
Sketch p. 39

Around 1900, Michael Cavanagh designed Perth's **Central Fire Station**. Like Temple Poole's Mint, it is built of rusticated limestone and, with its rounded arches, is essentially Romanesque. But this is an altogether more fanciful building.

Former **Albany Bell Tea Rooms**, c. 1896
(upper facade shown)
91 Barrack Street
Architect unknown

Peter Harper.

Cavanagh, possibly aided and abetted by his brother James, has thrown into it everything in the book. There are two turreted gables (both emblazoned with red fire helmets), a frieze above a central colonnade, recessed verandahs with iron lace, and even chimney stacks with terracotta pots. It is a visual delight.

With its rapidly expanding suburbs, Perth was now a good city for an entrepreneur with an eye to an empire. Albany Bell started small in 1893 with a confectionery business in Fremantle's High Street. Within fifteen years he was operating a large factory that manufactured the pastries and sweets on offer in all of his eleven tea rooms.

Albany Bell Tea Rooms
Sketch p. 41

The classically inspired facade of the Barrack Street **Albany Bell Tea Rooms** (c. 1896) is still recognizable.[18] On the first floor there is a row of arched windows punctuated by pilasters with Corinthian capitals. On the keystone of each arch is the face mask of a moustachioed gentleman. It is not unreasonable to suspect that the features are those of Albany Bell himself. It was Bell who introduced Perth and the goldfields to the delights of the American-style soda fountain and the ice-cream 'sundae'.

Barrack Street facades
Sketch opposite

Barrack Street still retains much of its gold rush character, although key buildings have been demolished and others have been tampered with or allowed to become run down. Three quite glorious turn-of-the-century facades can be observed by looking across from Governor Stirling's statue, including that of the former McNess Royal Arcade (1897). They demonstrate many of the decorative devices that were commonly found festooning

---

Three **Barrack Street facades**, late 1890s/early 1900s
Near corner Barrack and Hay Streets
Architects: Various, including William Wolf
Former McNess Royal Arcade (1897) right

Peter Harper.

Seeligson Loan Office
Sketch opposite

Barrack Street Bridge
Sketch p. 47

commercial buildings. Notable in the McNess building are the fanlight windows and the Corinthian pilasters.

At 143 Barrack Street is the former **Seeligson Loan Office**. It pre-dates the gold rush, but, with its elaborate decorative details, it clearly foreshadows the exuberance of 1890s architecture. Once in possession (as were many of Perth's commercial buildings) of a fine double verandah with cast-iron lace, it illustrates the importance placed on showing a bold face to the street. The wall bordering the laneway, by contrast, is devoid of decoration.

Taking Barrack Street across the railway line into Beaufort Street is the **Barrack Street Bridge**. Its lamps, emblazoned with black swans, date from 1894, when the original wooden bridge was reconstructed in steel and concrete.

One of the surprising stories associated with the Barrack Street Bridge involves Henry Lawson and his wife Bertha who, in 1896, were honeymooning in Perth. With the gold rush being at its height, there was a critical shortage of accommodation that was eased only when the authorities established camps, including one below the East Perth cemetery. The Lawsons had tramped through Perth, knocking on the doors of every hotel and guest house, and despite the fact that Henry was already a literary celebrity Australia-wide, no bed was to be had. Foot-weary and desperate, they camped for a night or two by the railway line, under the cover of the bridge. With one of Albany Bell's tea rooms just a little way up the street, we can be confident that the Lawsons were at least well fed.

Former **Seeligson Loan Office**, c. 1880s
143 Barrack Street
Architect unknown

BRIDAL FASHIONS
CASA DELLA SPOSA
BRIDAL FASHIONS
NO ENTRY
PETER HARPER

Settling into prosperity: 1901–1910

By the turn of the century, the euphoria of the gold rush had subsided, but there was no escaping the change that had been wrought. Professor J.M. Freeland, one of Australia's most influential architectural historians, summed it up like this:

> In 1892, Perth had been a primitive frontier town with all the rawness and lack of style of a pioneer settlement. By 1900, it had been dipped bodily into a bucket of pure Victoriana and taken out, dripping plaster and spiked with towers and cupolas in a bewildering variety of shapes, to dry.[19]

It was apt that the federation of the former Australian colonies should have more or less coincided with the death of Queen Victoria and the start of a new century. For Perth, the future seemed bright. Gold had settled into steady and profitable production, and the rural sector was doing well.

Supreme Court
Sketch p. 49

One of the first major buildings of the new century was John Grainger's **Supreme Court** (1902–03). Viewed from a distance through gaps in the Stirling Gardens foliage, it promises to be a neo-classical structure of fine proportions. But up close it is a disappointment. It would appeal more had it been of sandstone and granite construction, but after the huge public works programme brought on by the gold rush, the government coffers could stretch only to red brick and grey cement. And without steps sweeping up to the double-columned portico, it sits rather squatly on the ground.

Barrack Street Bridge lamps, c. 1894
Corner Barrack and Wellington Streets
Architect unknown

Peter Harper

Grainger, who had left a thriving practice in Melbourne to replace George Temple Poole as Chief Architect in 1897, was father to one of Australia's most unusual (and gifted) sons, the pianist and composer Percy Grainger. So perhaps we can forgive Grainger senior for the conservatism and uneven quality of his buildings. Forgiveness was not something he received from his wife, Rose, however. Percy Grainger's biographer presents the composer's father as sexually hyperactive, boastful of his conquests, and a heavy drinker prone to acts of violence. Worst of all, for Rose, he had infected her with the syphilis he had contracted from a prostitute. It was not a happy household. A permanent separation was brought about when Rose, convinced of her son's genius, took him off to Europe for specialist tuition. Without wife and son with him in Melbourne, Grainger accepted the Perth job.

During Grainger's frequent illnesses, his very able deputy, Hillson Beasley, took control of what was still a busy public works schedule, including the designs for Parliament House, the State Library, the Art Gallery, the Central Police Courts and the Central Police Station. One of the buildings Grainger managed to do at least some of the work on was the Government House Ballroom (1899). A few decades later, his celebrated son was to give a piano recital there.

In the 1890s, when Albany Bell was giving the citizens of the city tea and cake, another energetic entrepreneur was serving them beer and entertainment. He was Thomas Molloy, and a more industrious fortune-builder it would be difficult to imagine.

Supreme Court, 1902–03
Stirling Gardens, off Barrack Street
Architect: John Grainger

Peter Harper

He decided early on that property speculation was the way to a comfortable retirement. Hotels and theatres were his particular interest, and with the gold boom came William Wolf, an architect who would serve Molloy's penchant for the grand and ostentatious.

Wolf, the son of a New York architect, trained in Germany and worked in London before moving to Australia to try his luck in Melbourne and Sydney. In the 1890s, when the Eastern colonies were deep in recession, gold drew him to the West. At the time, Molloy was a long-standing Perth City Councillor (he served four terms as Mayor) and had just lost his seat in parliament as the Member for Perth. Wolf found Molloy keen to build a new hotel in central Hay Street, to which he ultimately wanted to add Perth's first full-scale live theatre.

The Hotel Metropole (incorporating the Theatre Royal) was the dress rehearsal for the Molloy-Wolf blockbuster of 1904, **His Majesty's Theatre** (and Hotel). Perth had not seen anything like it.

His Majesty's Theatre
Sketch opposite

At the intersection of Hay and King Streets, His Majesty's is akin to a big wedding cake iced with every classical device imaginable and topped with not two but six reclining lions. The programme notes for the opening night boasted that 'nearly four million bricks and over 300 tons of iron and steel have been used in its construction'. Built at a cost of £42,000, its horseshoe-shaped auditorium once seated a total of 2,584, on three levels. And for those balmy Perth evenings before the advent of air-conditioning, the dome could be winched open to reveal the

---

His Majesty's Theatre, 1904
Corner Hay and King Streets
Architect: William Wolf

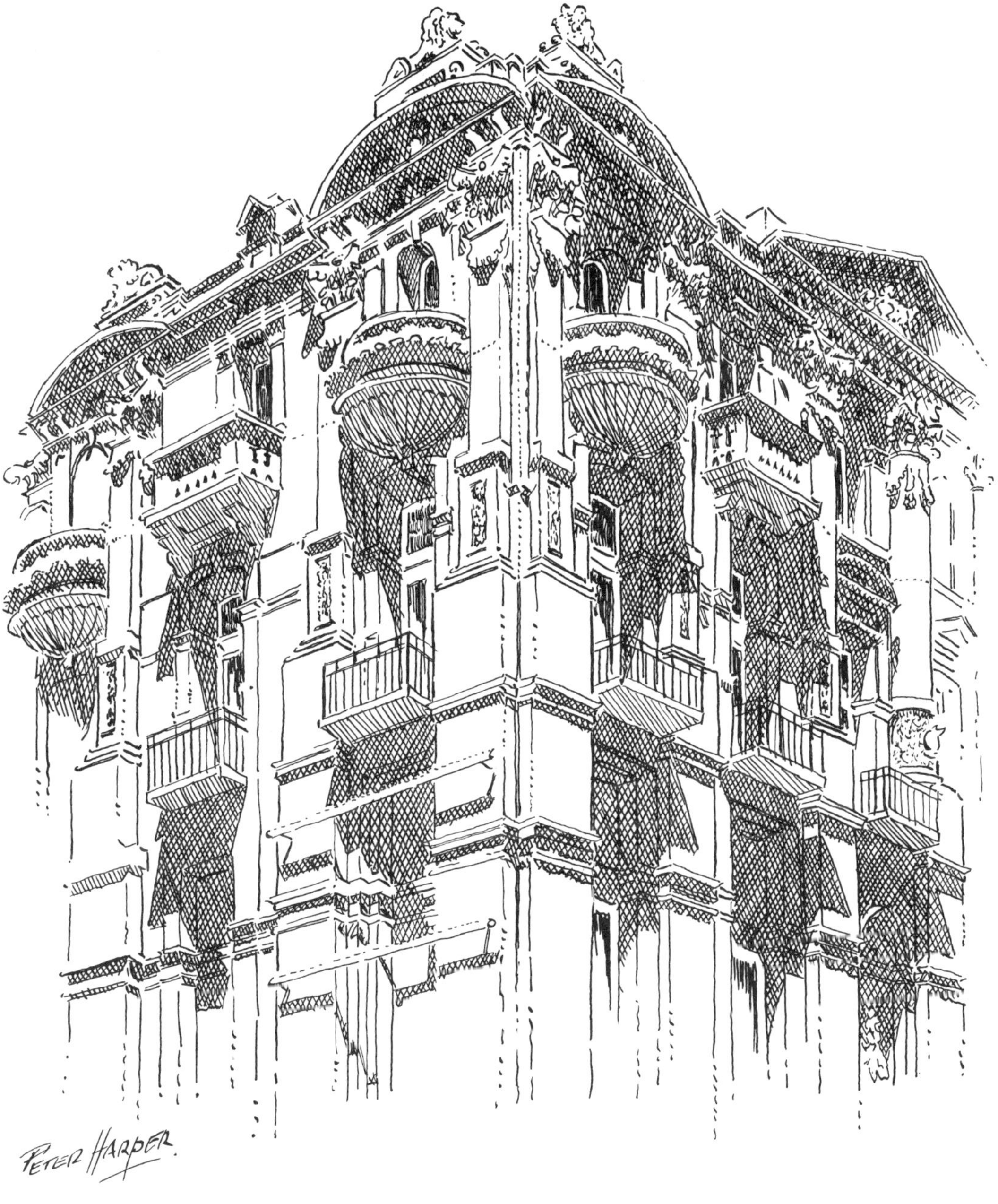
PETER HARPER

stars. Now lavishly restored, and seating fewer patrons in more generous rows, His Majesty's stands as Perth's most potent symbol of the buoyant, brash optimism that came with gold.

While His Majesty's is an enduring symbol of the entrepreneurial spirit of the era, many equally fine late-nineteenth and early-twentieth century commercial buildings were lost in the string of property booms that started in the late 1950s and were brought crashing down by the stock market collapse of 1987. Most of these buildings occupied key corner sites along St Georges Terrace, including Talbot Hobbs's glorious Moir Chambers, better known as the T & G Building. Opened in 1896 on the south-western corner of the Barrack Street intersection, it was not only Perth's first 'high rise' office building[20], but one of such visual splendour that if it stood today it would be lauded with a voice as strong as that which proclaims Temple Poole's Titles Office as one of our nation's more distinctive late Victorian buildings.

20 Howard Street
Sketch opposite

Howard Street was created in 1897 to provide an additional link between St Georges Terrace and The Esplanade, and by 1910, it was a little treasure trove of Victorian and Edwardian architecture. Only a block long and on a steep gradient, it quickly became a hub of the legal profession. Several prominent firms erected suitably solid and dignified chambers, including those at number 20. Built in 1905 for Haynes, Robinson & Cox, the initials of whom can be seen in the elaborate metal grill adorning the entrance, this is arguably Perth's most sophisticated example of the Gothic Revival style. The light honey colour of its facade is that of Donnybrook stone, the

---

20 Howard Street, 1905
Architect: Charles Oldham

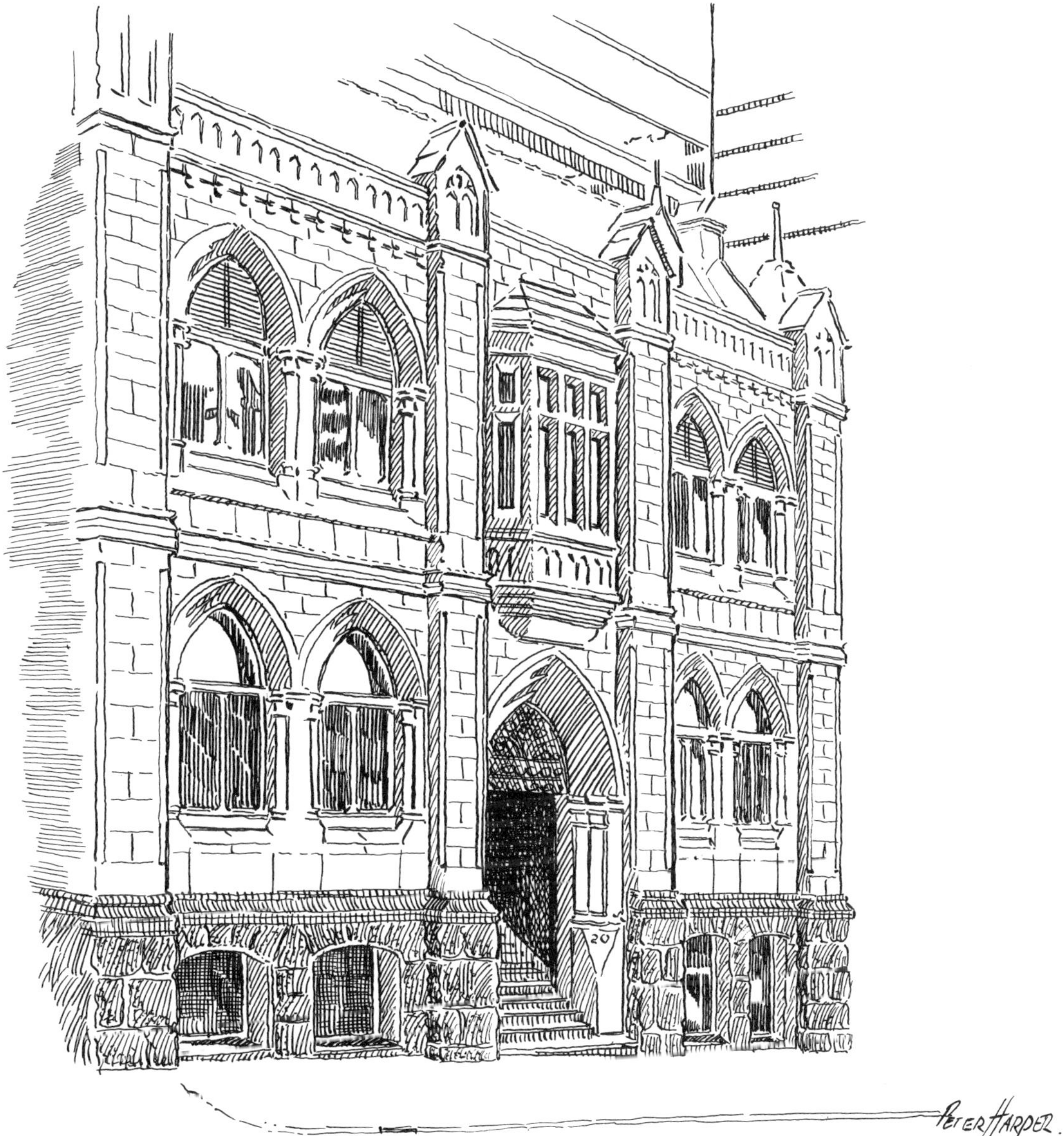
20
PETER HARPER.

prestige building material of the time. It was designed by Charles Oldham who, in a variety of partnerships, was one of the most admired and successful architects of the dozens who had been lured to Perth by the prospect of rich commissions.

There is a certain sadness that comes with the realization that, as with St Georges Terrace, only a handful of Howard Street's turn-of-the-century buildings remain intact. Most of its original structures had come from the design board of the Ballarat-born Oldham, offering a unique but now largely lost opportunity to gauge one man's craft across a variety of styles. Fortunately for the generations to come, King Street, another of Perth's small precincts, has survived largely unscathed. With its carefully-planned conservation, it provides a vibrant reminder of how things were.

Today's Perth offers sometimes striking, sometimes subtle contrasts between old and new. It seems that the 'knock it down' days that gained momentum in the 1960s have passed and there is a sympathetic re-evaluation taking place of what is left. But every day the remnants of the past become more precious, not always because they are universally accepted as fine structures in their own right, but because they help us to define who we are by showing us where we have been.

NOTES

1. Trollope, A., *Australia and New Zealand*, vol. 2, Chapman & Hall, London (1873), p. 128.

2. M.L. Freycinet, quoted in Peron, M.F., *A Voyage of Discovery to the Southern Hemisphere*, Richard Phillips, London (1809), p. 143.

3. Williams, A.E, *Western Australia — An Architectural Heritage*, Williams Pioneer Publications, Perth (1979), p. 42.

4. Stirling wanted to call the new colony Hesperia because it faced the westering sun.

5. Ticket-of-leave was a form of parole lasting from one to four years and ending in the ticket-of-leaver being granted a conditional pardon.

6. Hughes, Robert, *The Fatal Shore*, Pan Books, London (1988), p. 548.

7. ibid., p. 580.

8. Bricks may be laid so that either the short end or the long side is left exposed to view. Flemish bond involves alternating courses of 'headers' (short ends) and 'stretchers' (long sides).

9. Apperly, R., Irving, R., and Reynolds, P., *A Pictorial Guide to Identifying Australian Architecture*, Angus & Robertson, Sydney (1989), p. 82.

10. Arthur Bayley and William Ford discovered gold at Coolgardie in 1892, thus pioneering the gold rush to what became the 'Eastern Goldfields' of Western Australia. In July 1851, James Esmond won a cash reward for finding gold within 320 kilometres of Melbourne, Victoria's capital. His success sparked a major gold rush that transformed the colony.

11. During the 'Second Empire' of Napoleon III (1850–70), Paris was extensively remodelled under the direction of Baron Haussmann. The opulence of the 'new' Parisian architecture was copied world-wide.

12. Pitt Morison, M., and White, J., eds, *Western Towns & Buildings*, University of Western Australia Press, Perth (1979), p. 109.

13. To use a dolly, an ore-crushing device.

14. Stannage, C.T., *The People of Perth*, Perth City Council, Perth (1979), p. 230.

15. Western Australia's population grew from 46,290 in 1890 to 180,146 in 1900.

16. Apperly, Irving, and Reynolds, op. cit., p. 4.

17. Molyneau, I., *Looking Around Perth*, Wescolour Press, Perth (1981), p. 27.

18. Look above Hungry Jack's at 91 Barrack Street.

19. Freeland, J.M., *Architecture in Australia — A History*, Cheshire (1968), p. 198.

20. Moir Chambers had four full floors, and was capped with a corner turret that almost doubled its height.

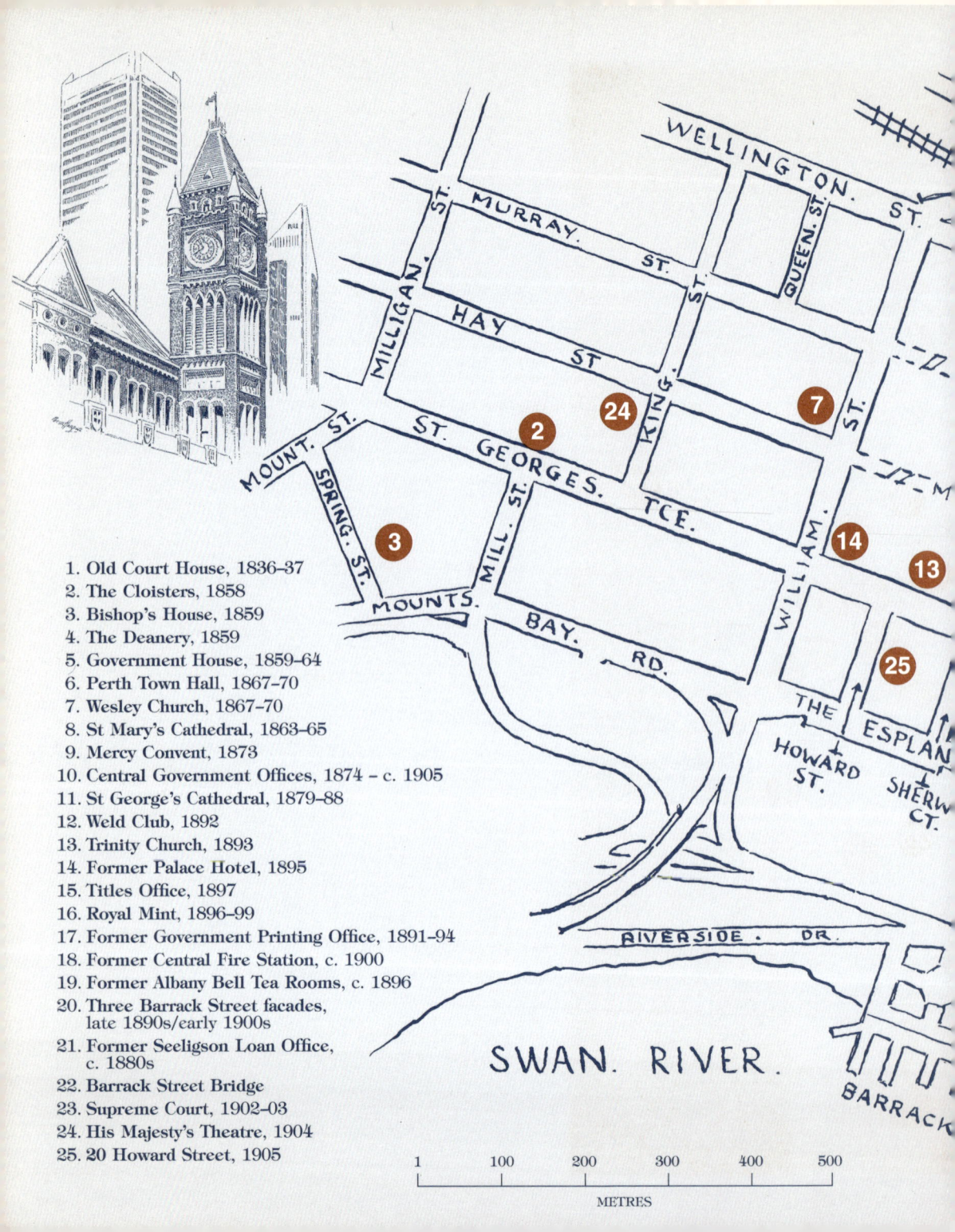

1. Old Court House, 1836-37
2. The Cloisters, 1858
3. Bishop's House, 1859
4. The Deanery, 1859
5. Government House, 1859-64
6. Perth Town Hall, 1867-70
7. Wesley Church, 1867-70
8. St Mary's Cathedral, 1863-65
9. Mercy Convent, 1873
10. Central Government Offices, 1874 – c. 1905
11. St George's Cathedral, 1879-88
12. Weld Club, 1892
13. Trinity Church, 1893
14. Former Palace Hotel, 1895
15. Titles Office, 1897
16. Royal Mint, 1896-99
17. Former Government Printing Office, 1891-94
18. Former Central Fire Station, c. 1900
19. Former Albany Bell Tea Rooms, c. 1896
20. Three Barrack Street facades, late 1890s/early 1900s
21. Former Seeligson Loan Office, c. 1880s
22. Barrack Street Bridge
23. Supreme Court, 1902-03
24. His Majesty's Theatre, 1904
25. 20 Howard Street, 1905